WHY BITCOIN?

WHY BITCOIN?

Tomer Strolight

© 2022 Tomer Strolight

WHY BITCOIN?

All Right Reserved.

Original cover design by Klaus Nordby

Typesetting and cover adaptation: Konsensus Network

ISBN 978-9916-697-94-8 Hardcover

978-9916-697-95-5 Paperback

978-9916-697-96-2 E-book

Konsensus Network ★ https://konsensus.network

The articles in this book were originally written and published individually on Medium.com and Swanbitcoin.com from March through May 2021.

CONTENTS

Preface i
1. Why Bitcoin Exists 1
2. Why Bitcoin is Unlike Anything You Have Ever Seen 5
3. Why Choose Bitcoin 7
4. Why It Takes Both Time and Effort to Make Bitcoins 9
5. Why You Do Not Need Permission To Use Bitcoin 11
6. Why Bitcoin's Rules Are Enforced by Math and Physics . 13
7. Why Nobody Can Stop Bitcoin 15
8. Why Bitcoin is the Path to Economic Stability 19
9. Why Bitcoin is The Way to Save Money 23
10. Why Bitcoin's Buying Power Keeps Rising 25
11. Why and How Bitcoin Uses Energy 27
12. Why Bitcoin's Energy Use Benefits Our Environment ... 31
13. Why Bitcoin is the World's Greatest Gladiator 35
14. Why Bitcoin Will End The Greatest Heist In History .. 39
15. Why Civilization Needs Bitcoin 45
16. Why Bitcoin is Changing the World 49
17. Why Bitcoin is the World's Most Inclusive Institution .. 51

18. Why Bitcoin Attracts Extraordinary Talent	53
19. Why You Shouldn't Fear Bitcoin	57
20. Why Bitcoin is So Complicated	61
21. Why Bitcoin Can Handle All the Commerce in the World	63
22. Why Bitcoin's Imitators Are Scams	67
23. Why Bitcoin is So Much More Than Money	71
24. Why You Need Bitcoin	73
25. Why Bitcoin is the New Frontier	75
26. Why Bitcoin is Worthy of Your Love	77
27. Why Bitcoin is a Movement of Peace	79
The Bitcoin White Paper	85
More from the Author	95

Preface

When I wrote these essays, they represented my debut into the Bitcoin content community. The entire collection was intended to fill a void. There were no short yet insightful reads about Bitcoin suited to both newcomers and experienced bitcoiners. I wanted to make some of the deepest and most important but unexplained and poorly understood aspects of Bitcoin accessible to all.

I sought to do this through short sentences, clever analogies, and a bit of whimsy, to keep it all in good fun – even though what I was discussing was very serious.

My goals were largely achieved. Many of these essays were shared widely on social media. The whole collection was turned into an ebook. Volunteers came forward to translate them into many languages. Guy "The Voice of Bitcoin" Swann, released them as an audiobook.

However, there was a weakness with the original collection. I initially published each essay as I wrote it – and I wrote them as they came to me. There was no rhyme or reason behind that order. I simply acted on my inspiration, not according to any plan.

This book remedies that. A book is linear. And its contents have a proper order. So creating this book required that I work out a logical order for the essays.

That is what I have done. The entire collection is now organized. For example, the online series ended with "Why Bitcoin Exists." That is now the first – because it answers the most basic question anyone should have about Bitcoin: "Why does this thing even exist?"

I am delighted with how it turned out. This book takes readers on a journey of what Bitcoin is, how it works, its impact on the world, and the personal impact Bitcoin will have on them. It does so without requiring knowledge of economics, math, politics, or computer science. Yet I have not shied away from tackling these areas — nor from topics like ethics and self-actualization.

In creating a physical book, for its debut, I also wanted it to be one that people displayed, read, and shared. I wanted it to be esthetically delightful in ways not possible in blogs.

To that end, I drafted my dear friend and gifted artist, Klaus Nordby, to design the book. He is uncompromising in making readable material beautiful. That coffee table version, filled with photos and color on every page, can be ordered via print on demand, in both softcover and hardcover, at blurb.com/user/TomerStrolig.

Klaus also acted as my editor. He ensured that each piece was intellectually precise and honest. We wrestled over the choice of crucial words. We worked together to find solutions for every challenge we discovered. It was an amazing creative experience for us both, which we both enjoyed and learned from. The original coffee table book also featured an original artwork by the artist known as Chiefmonkey, who created it as a laser-cut sculpture titled "SHAmanic Universal Consciousness" and auctioned it for sale at Bitcoin Miami. Portions of it are reproduced in chapter breaks here.

I want to pay thanks to Cory Klippsten and the whole team at Swan Bitcoin. Cory reached out to me when I was just starting the series and encouraged me to turn it into an ebook — which Swan promoted. They also provided financial support for the original print edition.

Finally, thanks to Niko Laamanen and everyone at Konsensus Network for their support and efforts in making this edition possible. Their efforts will ensure its contents are explored and evaluated by many inquisitive minds.

Preface

I dedicate this edition to everyone curious enough about Bitcoin to direct their time and energy to understanding it. It is an unexpected and unpredictable journey, about so much more than money. Hopefully this book can help those on this journey sort out some things along their way.

Tomer Strolight

February 25, 2023

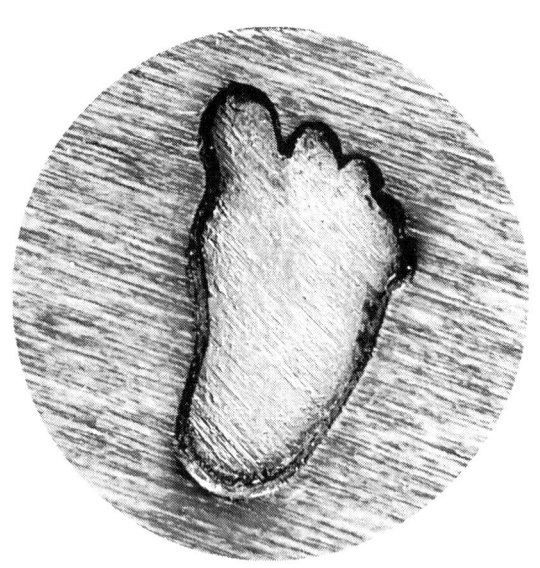

Chapter 1

Why Bitcoin Exists

What is the Purpose of Bitcoin?

Why did anyone bother to create bitcoin? What problems were they trying to solve? If you are new to the whole idea of a digital asset involving the mysterious field of cryptography, these are some questions that probably come to your mind.

Before you get caught up in asking if you can "get rich quick" from bitcoin, you should be asking if it has a deeper purpose. Bitcoin was created to serve a very specific purpose. If it did not serve that purpose, it would not be worth anything. Fortunately, it does. And, it was carefully and meticulously engineered to serve it precisely.

Bitcoin's purpose is to provide reliable money that will serve all mankind – forever. That is a pretty lofty goal: serving all of mankind, forever!

Was There Even a Problem in the First Place?

Is our money unreliable? Does it really fail to serve all mankind? Are its days numbered? The sad fact is that the answer to all these questions is "Yes!"

First, our money is unreliable: it loses its purchasing power through inflation. We also experience volatile economic cycles that destroy capital, jobs, wealth, and stability.

Next, our money does not serve all mankind – many middlemen charge excessive fees to store and send our money. It is expensive to use internationally since converting it to other currencies is costly. Many people in the world lack any access to reliable banking. Our money system serves elites far better than it serves ordinary people.

Finally, our money system is doomed to collapse. Currencies worldwide are rapidly losing purchasing power. In fact, throughout history, paper money decreed into existence by governments has failed every time that it has been implemented.

And sadly, we cannot turn back the clock and go back to a time when gold was money. Gold is simply not secure from seizure, and it is far too slow, difficult and expensive to transport in a global economy.

Bitcoin Fixes This

Bitcoin was created through an ingenious and unprecedented combination of technologies. It provides, for the first time ever, money that is reliable, that serves all mankind, and that will last forever.

Nothing like this has ever existed before. Bitcoin is free from inflation – its supply will never exceed 21 million coins. Each coin is divisible into 100 million units called satoshis. These will be issued on a fixed, unalterable schedule – taking over 100 years.

Bitcoin is for all mankind – there are no elites who can manipulate it. Unlike the currencies of our present money, nobody can create bitcoins effortlessly for themselves. Nobody can be prevented from using bitcoin – it will not allow anybody to stop someone else from using it. Finally, bitcoin is forever – its operation depends solely on the laws of physics and mathematics, and these laws will stay in effect – unaltered – for as long as the Universe exists.

Bitcoin was not created so that some people could "get rich quick". It was created to preserve the integrity of money – to make the most of your precious time, your energy, and your life.

With bitcoin you can keep what you have earned – and use it however, whenever, and wherever you desire. To you, bitcoin is reliable money that can serve you for the rest of your life – and it offers you an escape from being the victim of an unjust, broken, dying, and failing monetary system.

Chapter 2

Why Bitcoin is Unlike Anything You Have Ever Seen

Nothing like bitcoin has ever existed. Bitcoin is so different from anything ever seen before that it is necessary to begin our journey by describing what it is not.

Bitcoin is Unique

Bitcoin has no leaders, no employees, no headquarters, no offices, no government, no elections, no location, no property, no assets – and no money. It is not even incorporated or legally constituted in any place on Earth.

Bitcoin sees all of these things not only as unnecessary, but actually as undesirable. This is because bitcoin views all of these things not as strengths – but as vulnerabilities.

Bitcoin deals with such vulnerabilities in an elegant manner – simply by eliminating them. Were any of these features to be in bitcoin they would inevitably lead to the problems we see in all other institutions – such as being taken over, becoming corrupted, or being destroyed.

By removing these, bitcoin becomes uncontrollable, incorruptible, unstoppable – and indestructible. The elimination of these and all other vulnerabilities makes bitcoin invulnerable. All of these intentional omissions are the genius in its design which make bitcoin so indispensable and invaluable.

Perfection is achieved, not when there is nothing more to add, but when there is nothing left to take away.

– Antoine de Saint Exupery

Even More Things Bitcoin Does Not Do

Bitcoin does not keep track of the identities of the people or machines that use it – making it private. Bitcoin does not force itself on anyone – making it entirely consensual. Bitcoin does not exclude anyone from using it – making it universally inclusive. Bitcoin does not increase the supply of currency to meet rising demand – making it extremely precious.

Bitcoin is unlike anything you have ever seen. It needs to be, so it can provide humanity with the most perfect money that we will ever see.

Chapter 3

Why Choose Bitcoin

Why Should You Choose Bitcoin as Money?

The answer to this question lies in the fact that you can even ask it.

Let us recall, you are not asked to choose the dollar – nor the euro, the pound, the krone, the lira, the peso, the yen, and so on. You are born into a world where those currencies simply are your money and where the law orders you to accept them as money – and where everyone around you blindly accepts them as money. And so you, too, take it for granted that they are money. But if you look closely you'll see that the dollar isn't particularly fair money, or very good money, or very reliable money.

On the other hand, nobody has forced you, or anyone else, to use bitcoin. And no one ever will. So why should you start to think of it as money?

Bitcoin Asks that You Choose It

When it comes to the many necessary features of money – durability, divisibility, sendability, storability and many others – bitcoin is superior to either the dollar or to gold.

But more important than any one of those features is that bitcoin asks you to use it – instead of forcing you. You do not have to accept bitcoin, but you can – if you choose to.

Bitcoin Strives to Earn Your Choice

To become your money bitcoin needs to earn your well-deserved confidence – and the confidence of millions more people all over the world. Think of what must be true of bitcoin for it to become accepted by a hundred million people, and then a billion people – when each and every one must actually choose it.

Moreover, to remain your choice, bitcoin must always be the best choice – so that nothing better comes along to take its place. These two reasons – the need to earn your choice and to keep on earning it is what necessitates that bitcoin be the best money in the world. And, remarkably, since it is software, bitcoin can continuously adapt itself to provide all we need from our money.

Bitcoin Only Gets Better

These facts demonstrate how bitcoin is itself the ongoing process of becoming and remaining the very best, freely chosen money that can ever be. After all, how could either the dollar, which orders you to use it, or gold, which cannot improve itself, compete with bitcoin? Neither of them earn your choice. Whatever it is that people need from money, bitcoin is the only money in the world that can continuously improve and adapt to best suit those needs.

Bitcoin is Worthy

The very fact that bitcoin needs you to choose it means that it must become and remain worthy of your choice. As a result, bitcoin continuously improves to become better than any alternative. This creates a virtuous circle where bitcoin just keeps getting better, causing more people to choose it. And, with more people choosing it, bitcoin becomes even better money – which in turn gets more people to choose it, which makes it still better – and so on.

Chapter 4

Why It Takes Both Time and Effort to Make Bitcoins

You Work Hard for Your Money

To earn money you have to put in time and effort. So, for the sake of fairness, shouldn't it be the case that the creation of money itself also takes time and effort?

Yet, this is not the case with stateissued money. Any arbitrary amount of dollars, euros, pesos, pounds, and so on, can be conjured out of thin air instantly – and without effort.

This method of creating money without doing work discourages people from doing work for their money. Instead, it encourages people to seek handouts of this easily-produced money.

And, this isn't just welfare for the poor – it is mostly huge handouts for the very rich and politically connected.

Creating Bitcoins Takes Time

Bitcoin guarantees that its currency can only be created over a fixed schedule of time. Only a small amount of bitcoin is created, on average, every ten minutes. And that amount gets cut in half every four years. This leads to a maximum supply of 21 million bitcoins – ever.

Creating Bitcoins Takes Effort

Nobody can create bitcoins without proving that they worked to create them.

Bitcoins are created through a process named mining — because, like the actual mining of minerals, such as nickel, iron, and gold, real-world work must be done. This work is done by computers using electrical energy.

Many people compete to create new bitcoins. The more competitors there are, and the more work they do — the harder it becomes to win this competition. Each competition typically lasts around ten minutes and then restarts when one miner succeeds at this task.

Bitcoin is the only money that requires work to create and where the supply remains fixed no matter how much work goes into making it.

Fairly Balanced Money

Since you must put in your time and your effort to earn money, shouldn't you choose a money that also requires those who create it to put in their time and their energy?

That money is bitcoin.

Chapter 5

Why You Do Not Need Permission To Use Bitcoin

Bitcoin is Really for Everyone

Everybody may use bitcoin. Nobody's approval is needed to use it. And when I say nobody, I really mean it – not now, not ever!

Unlike all financial institutions, bitcoin doesn't want to know your name – it can't. It also does not want to know your gender, your age, your income, your race, your politics, your driving record, your debts, your kinks – or any other single thing at all about you.

If you can produce a large random number, then you can use bitcoin. Don't worry, you can generate such a number if you have access to a computer or phone – or even just a coin to toss, or some dice to roll.

Nobody is in Charge of Bitcoin

The reason you do not need anybody's permission to use bitcoin is because there is no one to ask. There is no one and nothing that can grant you permission – or refuse it. If you have some bitcoin you want to send to somebody else, they do not need any permission to use bitcoin either.

Why is Bitcoin Permission-less?

Bitcoin avoids any permission-granting requirement because it views the use of money as a universal human right.

As such, bitcoin does not want to know who you are, what you are buying, why you are sending the coins, where the recipient is – or anything else. You are free to do as you wish with your bitcoins!

Now, this idea may initially bother you a little bit. Doesn't this mean criminals can use bitcoin? Yes. And, it just so happens that criminals can use other forms of money, too. Criminals have existed since long before bitcoin was invented in the year 2009.

In many parts of the world, the real criminals are the tyrants in charge of the government who treat innocent civilians as criminals and violate their rights. Bitcoin can not judge anyone or anything and it remains completely neutral towards all comers.

Everyone, Everywhere – Forever

Bitcoin will work for anyone and everyone. It will work anywhere, wherever. Bitcoin will work anytime, forever. So if you are a carpenter in Zimbabwe now, you can use it. If you are an archaeologist in Antarctica in 200 years, you can too. Over time, countries will come and go, companies will come and go and rulers will come and go – but bitcoin will still be here, operating independently of whether any of these countries, companies, or rulers even exist.

How is Bitcoin Permission-less?

Bitcoin manages to be permission-less by excluding the very notion of users in its design. Bitcoin only cares whether the correct rules for spending bitcoins are followed. These rules are purely mathematical and bitcoin can verify and judge all transactions as either valid or not – true or false. Bitcoin is a transaction verification machine – not an identity-checker.

So I welcome you to use bitcoin – but of course, you do not need my permission.

Chapter 6

Why Bitcoin's Rules Are Enforced by Math and Physics

Nature's Laws Versus Man's Laws

The German Autobahn highways have no legally enforced speed limits. Only the laws of physics limit how fast automobiles can go. Consequently, the Germans have figured out how to make particularly fast cars — fast small cars, fast family cars, fast SUVs, fast trucks, and so on. And German cars are also especially safe fast cars, because nobody wants to die getting somewhere fast. This lack of regulations results in German cars being faster and safer than those made in countries where speed limits are set by government edicts.

This is also why bitcoin is the best money the world will ever see — because no government tells bitcoin what rules apply or how to enforce them.

To enforce its rules, bitcoin relies only on the laws of math and physics. These are eternal and unchanging laws. They are not made up on a whim. They cannot ever be changed — not by any individual or any group. This ensures that bitcoin's promises are as reliable as the laws of nature themselves.

How Bitcoin Uses Nature's Laws

Like the safety and speed goals of German cars, bitcoin has safety and speed goals too.

Safety-wise, bitcoin provides the monetary equivalent of safety — theft prevention — by allowing users to store their bitcoins where only they can find them. It accomplishes this by using astronomically large random numbers as the storage locations, like bank account numbers, but trillions and trillions and trillions times bigger. Physics dictates that nobody can guess these numbers even if they turned the whole planet into a giant computer making endless guesses.

As for speed, bitcoin does not try to go fast. Instead, it seeks to maintain a steady pace. The pace bitcoin maintains is that its miners discover and add one new block of transactions to its ledger — the blockchain — every ten minutes on average, forever. Bitcoin enforces this goal, too, using the eternal, unchanging laws of math and physics. If anyone turned all the world's energy towards trying to speed this up, bitcoin would slam on the brakes at a pre-set and frequently occurring milestone. Conversely, if anyone tried to slow this down, bitcoin would step on the accellerator and speed it up at that same milestone.

Achieving this average speed target relies on combining "Proof of Work," which is based on physical computing work that requires energy be spent in the real world with a few lines of computer code called the "Difficulty Adjustment." This is how bitcoin maintains its pace of block discovery.

Bitcoin Only Obeys Nature's Laws

No government edict can change any of this. Nobody and nothing can violate these mechanisms rooted in Nature itself — no protester, no banker, no lawmaker, no hacker, no corporation, no government, no army — no attacker of any kind.

With bitcoin you can count on math and physics — instead of the promises of bureaucrats and politicians — to protect your savings.

Chapter 7

Why Nobody Can Stop Bitcoin

Just about every man-made thing can be stopped – somehow. We can slam on a vehicle's brakes. We can cut a machine's power. We can order an organization stopped – by the armed forces, if necessary. It seems like you can stop anything with some force that counteracts whatever keeps that thing going.

But bitcoin is unstoppable. So exactly how does bitcoin manage to be unstoppable? Bitcoin employs two primary countermeasures to ever being stopped.

Flawless Replicas Everywhere

Bitcoin's first defence against being stopped is that you cannot actually locate it. It is impossible, after all, to stop something that you cannot find. Every bitcoin node is an instance of the bitcoin program running on some computer. And each node is an exact replica of every other one. Each node contains all the programming necessary to run bitcoin – along with all the addresses of every portion of every bitcoin.

To stop bitcoin would require stopping each and every node, everywhere in the world, and keeping them all stopped – forever.

However, bitcoin is very easy to run. It can operate on even the most basic of computers available today. So, large numbers of people do run it. Bitcoin nodes can also hide their location so that nobody can see where they are running. Therefore, it is impossible to find all the computers in the world running bitcoin.

If anyone, even the government, was trying to hunt down all these nodes in an attempt to stop bitcoin, they would fail. They might find some nodes, or maybe even a lot of them, but as long as bitcoin is running somewhere on Earth, on some computer – it is still running.

Even if an attacker managed to stop every node for a time, as soon as any node resumed – bitcoin would continue exactly where it left off. In fact, the first thing every node does when it resumes running is to make itself into a precise replica of all the other nodes.

There are tens of thousands of bitcoin nodes – running everywhere, all over the world, right now. There is no way to know exactly how many. That alone makes it impossible to know how hard a task it is to stop bitcoin.

Flexible Energy Requirements

Bitcoin's second defense is how it uses energy.

Most things require some minimum amount of energy to operate. Bitcoin has no such minimum. Yes, bitcoin does use energy – to ensure that no node can deceive any other node about the true state of the network. The correct ledger is the one with the most energy used.

But precisely how much energy bitcoin needs is regularly adjusted, through the Difficulty Adjustment, by bitcoin itself – and there is no minimum absolute value needed. If anyone managed to cut power from all but one of the nodes, eventually, bitcoin would adapt. Through this mechanism, bitcoin's energy requirements would simply diminish to the point that just one node's power would be all that was needed to keep the network operating. So bitcoin cannot be starved of the energy it needs, because it can operate on just a tiny amount – if that is all it can get.

UnFindable + UnStarvable = UnStoppable

Put these two defenses together and what you are left with is unstoppability. Since nobody can find all the nodes that exist and nobody can starve it of the energy it needs — nobody can stop bitcoin!

Chapter 8

Why Bitcoin is the Path to Economic Stability

There is No Reliable Stability in National Currencies

In 2021, the Venezuelan Bolivar lost 99% of its value against the US dollar. Even the British Pound experienced 17% volatility in ups-and-downs relative to the US dollar in the same period. In fact, when it comes to how they function, national currencies offer very little security, usability, predictability, and, indeed, stability:

- None offer much predictability of their supply – and many, including the dollar, have seen massive supply increases in recent times.

- None are entirely resistant from theft by crooks or seizure from authorities.

- None are fully permission-less – regulations exist that require owners to identify themselves and declare their intended uses.

- All of them operate only within specific jurisdictions.

- And none can have their supply verified independently – it is doubtful if even the authorities in charge of them know what supply exists.

In summary, national currencies are not very stable at all.

WHY BITCOIN?

Yet, Bitcoin is Accused of Being Unstable

"Bitcoin is extremely volatile" claim journalists, economists and bankers. It is no wonder that they draw these conclusions when judging bitcoin by the standard of unstable national currencies.

Consider, however, if you were on a boat that was being tossed about by rough seas and were looking at a lighthouse on the shore. That lighthouse's position would appear "extremely volatile" – despite the fact that the lighthouse was perfectly stable.

Here is why bitcoin is actually like that lighthouse.

Bitcoin is Profoundly Stable Every detail in bitcoin is the very essence of stability. No matter what the world has thrown at it, bitcoin has kept all its promises:

- It has issued a precisely predictable supply exactly according to schedule.
- Its security has never been breached.
- It has allowed anyone in the world to use bitcoin.
- It has allowed owners to spend their coins without restrictions.
- It has allowed anyone in the world with a basic computer to verify its supply for themselves – without having to trust anybody else.

There have been no exceptions. Bitcoin is therefore extremely stable.

Bitcoin's Adoption is a Migration Towards Stability

When critics call bitcoin volatile, it is not meant to be a compliment. They are implying that stability is preferable to volatility. This much is correct. They are just mistaken about what stability is. Bitcoin's incredible stability and reliability is precisely what is attracting ever-growing numbers of people, corporations, institutions and governments to adopt it to ever-greater degrees.

As bitcoin's adoption increases, its value, as measured in dollars, rises profoundly — albeit with wild short-term fluctuations in its dollar-denomiated price.

But there is nothing about bitcoin's actual nature that is fluctuating. Just like a lighthouse, bitcoin remains perfectly stable.

In light of all this, it is no surprise that bitcoin is increasingly being chosen in place of national currencies. Bitcoin's steady and unbreakable assurances give the world a standard upon which we can trade with each other — across any distance, in any amount, and over any period of time.

Bitcoin's reliability is leading the world on a path towards greater economic stability.

Chapter 9

Why Bitcoin is The Way to Save Money

What Does "Saving Money" Mean?

Is saving money putting dollars into a savings account? Let us take a closer look at this familiar two-word phrase, "saving money."

The word "save" actually has two meanings. The first is "to store". The second is "to rescue". This second, to rescue, is the one we want to examine.

Next, what about the definition of "money"? Permit me to offer one, because dictionaries presume money is "physical coins or banknotes" – and that is outdated even before you consider the existence of bitcoin.

I propose simply that "money is an instrument that people use to store and transfer economic value."

Now, imagine if this instrument that people used to store and transfer such value was dying. We would need to rescue this instrument. We would need to save this instrument. We would need to save money.

So you see, when I talk about saving money, I do not mean "putting dollars into a savings account". I mean finding a new instrument that humankind can rely on to store and transfer economic value.

The reason we need this new instrument is because the old one is failing. For at least fifty years, government-issued money has been losing its abilty to store and transfer economic value through inflation.

A can of soup used to cost ten cents – now it costs a dollar. A house has gone up tenfold in price. Everything has gotten more expensive – in dollars.

Inflation occurs when the people who can create money abuse that power. Today, that abuse has reached a boiling point where trillions of dollars are created overnight, multiple times a year. This destroys savings held in alleged "savings" accounts.

Inflation is the money-killer.

Enter Bitcoin – Saving Money!

Bitcoin is here to rescue the very idea of money from destruction. It eliminates anyone's power to inflate away the savings of everyone.

In bitcoin, there is no inflation.

Remember, there will only ever be 21 million coins, each divisible into 100 million parts called "satoshis". These will be released according to an unchangeable schedule over the next 100+ years. This money will only be issued to people who put in the hard work to earn it.

This guaranteed scarcity, combined with the requirement to do work for newly-issued bitcoins, reintroduces integrity into the monetary system – thereby saving it from collapse.

However, it does so only for the monetary instrument which has these characteristics – and that instrument is bitcoin.

So bitcoin is literally here to save money from destruction. And if you want to save your money from destruction you should convert it to bitcoin.

Chapter 10

Why Bitcoin's Buying Power Keeps Rising

You work. You get paid – with money. You trade your money for the work that other people do. That is how they get paid.

But ask yourself: Over time, does the money you get paid with buy more of the work other people do, or does it buy less?

If you use your nation's currency, the answer is that inflation reduces what your money can buy. The money supply is growing more than the amount of work that is being done – so more money buys less work.

Some people try to avoid inflation by choosing to hold precious metals, like gold. The theory behind this is that gold's purchasing power should remain stable – since mining it requires work that is, for the most part, steady over time.

However, bitcoin's purchasing power just keeps going up. A lot. Why? Well, imagine if everything about the current process of creating money was flipped upside-down. Imagine a system that made it impossible to produce money by decree. Imagine a system that required real, hard work to create money.

Imagine that no matter how much work was put in, only a fixed quantity of money could be created in any given period of time. Imagine if that fixed quantity kept getting reduced.

Surely then, if all these things were true, money thus created would experience the opposite effects than the money that keeps losing purchasing power.

WHY BITCOIN?

When you use bitcoin, you choose this exact process of money creation — one that does not cause purchasing power to shrink over time, but rather, one where it grows.

All the things this article asked you to imagine are in fact true of bitcoin: it cannot be produced by decreee, its creation requires real, hard work, only a preset quantity is produced in any given time, and that quantity keeps getting reduced periodically.

This is why bitcoin's purchasing power keeps rising.

Chapter 11

Why and How bitcoin Uses Energy

How Does Bitcoin Use Energy?

Let me count the ways. First, bitcoin uses energy to prevent anyone from erasing any of its records.

If you own some bitcoin, that is because someone sent it to you. That transaction was recorded in the blockchain – the full history of the ownership of all bitcoins. If it were possible to erase that record then you would not own that bitcoin anymore. However, replacing records requires using more energy than has been used since they were created. To erase a transaction created a year ago requires more energy than has been used since. The older a transaction is, the more difficult it is to ever erase it.

Second, bitcoin uses energy to prevent anyone from passing off falsified records. Bitcoin has a way of checking how much energy has been used to create its blockchain at any given point in time. If anyone tries to pass off a fake blockchain, they would need to put more energy into it than the true one. The higher the energy requirement, the harder and more expensive this becomes.

Falsified records are easily invalidated by everyone, and the one true version of the blockchain remains in place.

When new blocks are discovered by miners, the highest-proof-of-work test is what all bitcoin nodes use to prove which one is valid. Any disputes between two versions are ultimately settled by which one contains the most work. The strongest one wins!

These energy requirements prevent anyone from re-spending coins that were previously spent. This is bitcoin's solution to the infamous "double-spend problem" – which had stymied all computer scientists until Satoshi Nakamoto published his bitcoin Whitepaper in 2008.

Bitcoin's Energy Use Eliminates Dependency on Human Authorities

It does not take much energy to participate in bitcoin. Anyone in the world can make a copy of the blockchain, keep it up to date, and ensure it is perfectly flawless. To verify everything, bitcoin relies only on computations that can run on ordinary computers – so anyone can check everything for themselves.

Because it is practical for anyone to verify for themselves, this proof-of-work method of determining validity eliminates needing to put trust in any human authority. This is the only known method for achieving perfect, world-wide agreement, free from any human authority.

Why Do People Put Energy into Bitcoin?

Bitcoins are very scarce. There will only ever be 21 million. This scarcity makes them increasingly valuable. Energy is not free. But there are people who choose to use costly energy to create valid, new blocks. This is how they earn newly created bitcoins.

Simply put, the bitcoin system pays people with bitcoins to put energy into reinforcing the security of bitcoin's history and adding to it.

How It All Comes Together

Bitcoin pays people with scarce money to do work. That work adds security to the money. Everyone who uses that scarce money benefits from this work – because it makes their scarce money even more secure.

This creates a virtuous circle, where work pays for more security, and where more security increases the value of the money that pays for the work, to increase its security.

Bitcoin's energy use is an integral and irreplaceable aspect of its operation. It uses energy to ensure agreement, validity, security, and scarcity to a degree nothing else on Earth provides – leading to the creation of the best money in history.

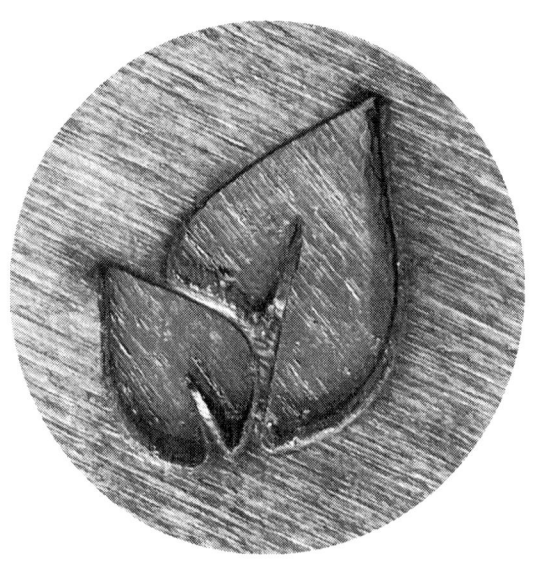

Chapter 12

Why Bitcoin's Energy Use Benefits Our Environment

Human Civilization Needs Energy

Harnessing energy is the essence of a flourishing human civilization on Earth. Without abundant energy, our lives would be cold, short, and miserable. And, there would be far fewer of us — which would be sad.

Bitcoin Prefers the Cleanest Energy

Bitcoin uses electricity as the energy in its mining process. There are many ways to generate harmless, clean electricity, including nuclear, hydro, wind, and solar. These sources of electricity are actually cheaper on-the-margin than fossil fuels. This is because none of them require costly extraction and transportation of millions of tons of fuel.

Bitcoin mining is a brutally competitive business. Thus, out of economic necessity, miners must use the cheapest sources of electricity available.

And, since the cheapest forms of electricity are also the cleanest, bitcoin miners are compelled to use these clean sources.

Bitcoin is a Worthy Use of Energy

Bitcoin does use plenty of energy. And, it is completely transparent about how much energy it uses. It does not try to conceal its energy use. This transparency makes it an easy target to criticize. Just imagine if other institutions, like banking and government, were equally transparent about their energy use!

Bitcoin's energy use provides a value that nothing else in the world can. It is global, reliable, secure, and sound money. It is far superior to our current system of money. And this is priceless.

Bitcoin Encourages Responsible Energy Use

Because bitcoin increases in value over time it encourages saving and discourages waste. These incentives reduce the irresponsible spending that inflationary currencies cause — expenditures which waste energy and pollute our environment.

Bitcoin Stabilizes Our Access to Energy

Electric power plants produce a largely steady stream of energy. However, our demand for electricity varies greatly during the day, and throughout the seasons: When we sleep, we turn off the lights, and use less electricity. When the weather is extreme, we turn on our heaters and air conditioners, using more electricity. This variance is inconsistent with how power plants and grids work.

Now, for the first time in history, there is a fix for this imbalance: bitcoin mining!

Mining allows power plants to operate at peak efficiency — independently of our fluctuating demands.

Further, mining pays for power that would be otherwise wasted. This improves the economics for both plant operators and their customers — it stabilizes supply, demand, and prices.

Bitcoin mining thereby improves the economics of clean energy — which benefits us and our environment.

Bitcoin Grows Our Access to Energy

By improving the economics of clean energy production, bitcoin actually encourages the building of more and larger clean power plants — displacing the use of older, dirtier plants.

In fact, bitcoin even makes possible the construction of clean power facilities that would otherwise not be built, which would leave people to use dirtier substitutes. This is especially true for small, remote populations that must rely on smallscale, dirty sources of electricity — such as diesel generators.

Because bitcoin mining can pay for any amount of electricity production, it now can make sense to build clean plants that otherwise would not have been economical to construct. For example, clean, volcanic geo-thermal energy in El Salvador is being used in bitcoin mining — well ahead of any of the local population's demand for that electricity.

Bitcoin radically changes our energy landscape for the better.

Chapter 13

Why Bitcoin is the World's Greatest Gladiator

Bitcoin Confronts Endless Attacks

Bitcoin has many enemies who would like to put an end to it – and they keep trying. Nations, companies, and hackers have all made attempts at this. Journalists have repeatedly declared bitcoin dead.

However, the reports of its death have been greatly exaggerated. And, in fact, bitcoin actually gets stronger each time someone tries to kill it. It even benefits from people trying to ban it. And it also welcomes all attempts to replace it with anything allegedly better.

When it comes to attacks on bitcoin, the question is not "what's going to kill bitcoin?" – rather, it is "how will this make bitcoin bigger, stronger, better, and more valuable?"

Bitcoin Thrives When Attacked

Satoshi Nakamoto created bitcoin with many capabilities that defend it against attacks that would damage or destroy any person, company, or country. And yes, bitcoin can survive even a nuclear attack.

In addition, bitcoin can also develop new defences that it previously lacked. Because it is software, it can add and adopt new capabilities – and it highly incentivizes the people who own bitcoins to create and install such defensive capabilities.

Bitcoin is the Greatest Gladiator the World Has Ever Seen

Like the Ancient Roman gladiators who fought publicly and to the death at the Colosseum, all of bitcoin's battles take place out in the open. Each time bitcoin successfully fends off a new attack in the real world, everyone stands witness to its invulnerability from that threat.

As a result, all can then see for themselves, and tell the tale to others that bitcoin has, yet again, proven itself to be stronger than anything its attackers could come up with.

Bitcoin Grows From Being Attacked

One of the most significant ways bitcoin actually grows is by proving itself capable of adapting to and surviving attacks.

Many corporations and institutions that once attacked bitcoin are now beginning to store their wealth in bitcoin precisely for this reason: they had expected bitcoin to die, because they tried to kill it themselves — but they failed. These former enemies learned a valuable lesson: "If you can't beat them, join them." In then adopting bitcoin, they make it even more valuable and widespread.

The same lesson is learned by those who create and invest in competitors they expect will kill bitcoin. Most of these attempts failed miserably, because they are inferior to bitcoin.

But were they to offer an actual improvement, bitcoin could then be modified to implement that improvement. This would neutralize any temporary advantage the competitor might have.

Not every attack is easily defeated. Bitcoin has been through some very frightening and drawn-out battles. The most severe of these occurred when leading companies in the bitcoin ecosystem attempted to seize control of bitcoin. Yet, even in this worst-case example, bitcoin, the undefeatable gladiator, was victorious against their attacks.

It dealt a harsh and unequivocal lesson to all involved — enemy and ally alike — that absolutely nobody can take control of bitcoin!

Bitcoin Only Defends, it Never Attacks

Even when under attack bitcoin allows everyone to use it, including those who are attacking it.

Bitcoin's means of dealing with attacks is to survive them — without retaliation. It does not attempt to harm or kill its enemies.

Every design decision in bitcoin prioritizes only survivability. Any attacker is always welcome to halt their attack and, if they so choose, to embrace bitcoin in peace. Nobody is ever discriminated against by bitcoin for any past transgression.

Attack bitcoin, please!

This article is not meant to discourage anyone from attacking bitcoin if they think they have some clever idea. Instead, it throws down the gauntlet and invites them to do battle with bitcoin, the greatest gladiator the world has ever seen.

After all — it will only make bitcoin stronger.

Chapter 14

Why Bitcoin Will End The Greatest Heist In History

Time-Travelling Thieves

Here is a cool idea for a movie: Criminals from the past obtain a time machine and travel to the present where they steal money — which they then take back to the past. Their victims are helpless. The criminals cannot be sued by the victims because these thieves exist only in the victims' pasts.

Furthermore, the victims cannot remember they ever even had that stolen money — they are just poorer. But the victims do know they have been robbed because the crooks leave a trail where the only possible explanation is that someone from the past stole this money.

Everyone can tell they have been robbed because they each owe money for things they never bought. They simply find themselves owing money for things that were consumed by someone else — before they were even born. It therefore must be that someone in the past bought something the victims are now on the hook for.

Ready to have your mind blown? This-money stealing time machine and the crooks who use it actually exist in the real world. The crooks used it in the past to steal from you and there are more crooks like them in the present using it right now to steal from people in the future.

We can see the unmistakeable mark of this crime: every person now born owes money for things they never bought and will never get to use.

How Time-Theft Works

This money-stealing time machine is called "government deficits and debt". Each annual theft is called the deficit, and the total amount stolen throughout history is called the debt.

Now, there is nothing wrong with borrowing money — if you have the intention and the means to pay it back.

However, if you intentionally deceive the lender by spending the borrowings without having any intention to pay them back — you are committing fraud.

If you act even more outrageously by borrowing money which you say someone else will pay back which he does not even know you borrowed — you would be committing a double fraud.

Yet, this is precisely what government deficits are. Politicians keep borrowing but never paying back what they borrowed. None of them ever had any intention of paying it back. None of them ever have paid it back.

And worse, they do not personally assume any responsibility for paying it back, but instead make their debts the obligations of future generations. Clearly, these generations could not have agreed to taking on these debts — because they were not even born yet!

Every baby born in the United States today is immediately saddled with a debt of over $80,000 — which they obviously never agreed to.

Somehow, nobody gets arrested for this monstrous fraud. Nobody who commits it is made to repay the money they stole — nor are they jailed for their crimes. Why?

Maybe it is because everyone who should put a stop to the crime is an accomplice to it. The police are paid with this stolen money. The judges are paid with it. The prosecutors are paid with it. The lawmakers are paid with it. Even the recipients of government benefits are paid with it. So are the banks that loan it – to people who then find themselves even more hopelessly in debt.

Our system of money is so thoroughly corrupted that stealing from unborn children has become so commonplace that it is expected at all levels of the government.

Future-Theft of More than Money

In stealing money from our future the thieves are also stealing the sustainability of our civilization.

Like a bank robber flush with ill-gotten loot, easy money leads to irresponsible, short term consumption – without regard for long term consequences.

Our economy thus becomes overheated and exhausted – as we make negligent decisions that we would otherwise not have made.

And how do you think one overheats and exhausts an economy? Why, of course, with money stolen from the future!

The Cost of Short-Term Focus

Since 1971, politicians have been hell-bent on maximizing immediate consumption. They have achieved that goal through reckless, fraudulent borrowing from our future.

They panic if even one month goes by without "economic growth". If there are six such consecutive months in a row, they call it a "recession".

They use this to justify further theft from the future – without any regard to paying back that money or to the consequences this will have on civilization's long term health.

Why do we steal what we do not need or want? Why doesn't the madness of stealing from our future and destroying our civilization stop? It is because our money system is broken.

It was broken on the day it was created. That day was August 13, 1971. Suddenly then, money all around the world ceased being tied to the supply of gold. Instead, it could be printed by bureaucrats and politicians – and imposed as debts upon the people of the future.

The US president at the time was Richard M. Nixon – who is best known for saying "I am not a crook!"

In fact, however, he was such a grand crook, that even though he disgracefully resigned from office in 1974 – people being born today still owe money he stole from them before they were even born.

If Nixon had told the truth and understood what he had actually done, he would have said, while holding both his hands up in a gesture of victory, "I am the greatest crook in history!"

What Do We Need To End This Money-Madness?

Our kleptomaniacal system of money is an existential threat to civilization – and an affront to basic decency and justice.

We cannot go back to the system that existed before. That predecessor was called the "gold standard." That system failed.

Gold has been used as money throughout much of history, but it has an Achilles heel – a vulnerability that has been exploited repeatedly. The weakness of gold is that it can be seized by physical force. And this fact invites violence and incentivizes war.

The evidence: The Federal Deficit per year – also known as the amount stolen from the future – the heist begins in 1971 and reaches over $3 trillion in 2021 alone.

Consider this brief history of gold recounted by Michael Saylor in his debate on bitcoin versus Gold:

> *Gold invites violence. Alexander the Great gallivanted around the world to seize gold. Libby tells the story of a thousand Roman sieges to steal the gold. Caesar sacked Gaul to take their gold. Kublai Khan seized the gold. Pizarra seized the gold from the Incas. Cortez seized gold from the Aztecs. Charles I seized the gold from all the British nobles. The Prussians seized gold from the French in 1871. In World War One everybody seized gold. Lenin seized gold from the church in 1922. Roosevelt seized everybody's gold in 1933. Stalin seized the gold of the Spaniards in 1936. Churchill took everybody's gold in 1940 at the onset of World War Two. In 1944, at Bretton Woods the United States seized the world's gold and then took it hostage. Finally, Nixon 'killed' all the hostages in 1971. Gold is always getting seized."*

Despite retaining its value over long periods of time, all too often throughout history, the actual ownership of gold changed hands through physical seizure — rather than through voluntary exchange.

Bitcoin Disables the Money-Stealing Time Machine — Forever

Finally, there now exists a solution to all this. For the first time in history, a system of money has been engineered to solve the weaknesses of all previous systems. It solves the problems with gold — which invited violence and war. It solves the problems with debt-based money — which invites time-theft and short-sightedness.

This perfectly-engineered system is bitcoin. We do not have to let anyone steal from our children's future — or ruin our civilization any more, ever again.

WHY BITCOIN?

Unlike gold, bitcoin is unseizable. Neither all the military power in the world nor all of its computing power can seize even a single bitcoin. Nor can any forces borrow non-existent and never-to-exist bitcoins — claiming future generations will pay off this debt.

When the "bitcoin standard" replaces debt-based money, all of these destructive effects will cease. We will all then benefit from an economy that is permitted to cool down when overheated. We will benefit from a civilization where new efficiencies are not pilfered away on unnecessary "stimulus". We will benefit from bitcoin's incentives to generate abundant, clean energy.

Bitcoin will rid the world of the institutions and practices that dared to steal from the helpless, unborn citizens of the future. It will bring about the end of the greatest-heist ever that was foisted upon the whole world on that dark day in August of 1971.

Only one champion can defeat these wicked enemies of humanity perpetrating the greatest heist in all history — the world's greatest gladiator, bitcoin!

Chapter 15

Why Civilization Needs Bitcoin

The Magical Miracle of Money

Money is a tool unique to humans. It coordinates our activities and allows for voluntary co-operation on a vast and global scale. The results are extraordinary. Think about any product that you recently bought. Consider how many people worked to get the materials for it, manufacture it, package it, warehouse it, stock it and ship it. Yet you didn't have to talk to a single one of them. You just had to hand over some money to one business – and you didn't have to worry about any of these details.

This complex coordination of activities made easy by money is far beyond what anyone can plan. When seen in this way, money seems magically miraculous.

Money Creates Civilizations

With sound money, humans can create civilizations! Such societies offer people the means to satisfy their needs, wants, and values. Over time, civilizations achieve ever greater accomplishments through money's ongoing, magicalseeming powers of coordination.

Civilization's Destroyer – Dark Magic Money

Unfortunately, there are people who meddle with money and its magnificent co-ordination properties.

WHY BITCOIN?

Thieves try to obtain money through physical force. Frauds obtain it by promising something but not delivering on the promise. Politicians think they can better co-ordinate human action than money by forcing their preferences on others.

And then there are the central banks. They monopolize and control money itself — distorting and destroying its magical benefits. Our money has been completely under their control since 1971, with devastating consequences. For most people reading this, that means you have lived under their dark spell your whole life.

They claim that money should lose purchasing power over time. If money isn't losing enough purchasing power quickly enough, they act to destroy it faster. Their claim is that this will make people consume more quickly — which will be good for the economy.

They use their control over money to fuel this unnecessary, unwanted short term consumption by destroying people's ability to save for the long term.

The father of their movement, John Maynard Keynes, justified this great evil by saying "In the long term, we are all dead."

In the Long Term We Can and Should Thrive

However, we are not all dead in the long term. First, we each live longer, healthier and happier lives when we are able to focus on and plan for the long term. Eating well, exercising, and developing preventions and cures for diseases all extend our individual lives. Saving sound money for our future lets us live free of anxiety about it.

By moderating short term consumption, we preserve scarce resources and our environment for the future of all the people who will ever live.

Such long term focus allows us to embark on multi-generational projects. These were common in the age before central banks. But now, the world has been robbed of them.

Magic Internet Money to the Rescue

Sound money that allows humanity to co-ordinate its activities peacefully over the long term is desperately needed — it is good for individuals, for humanity, and for our environment.

Bitcoin is this money.

Bitcoin is not controlled by anyone — and it is built to last for the ages. Bitcoin is the invention we need to recover from the selfdestructive, short term, and inhuman forces that are casting darkness over our beautiful civilization.

Chapter 16

Why Bitcoin is Changing the World

Money Sometimes Changes Form

Since the dawn of civilization, money has been essential to society. As civilizations advanced, the instruments people used for money progressed along with it. People once used seashells, then beads, then salt, and then metal coins as money.

Today, the most common instrument used is government-issued paper money and its digital equivalents. Examples include the US dollar, Mexican peso, and the Euro.

Each time the form of money changed, the people who had lots of the old form went from being very wealthy, to having a bunch of worthless seashells, beads, piles of salt, antique coins – or stacks of worthless paper.

The Next Change is Happening Now

What we currently use as money is losing its integrity and many people are now looking for a better alternative.

In some cases, these national currencies have already failed – or are clearly headed in that direction.

Many people are discovering that bitcoin is the better alternative. More and more people are coming to the conclusion that bitcoin is their preferred money. Some choose it because its rules are incorruptible. Others because it keeps becoming more valuable. Many more because they see it is as a path to long term economic stability. And, even more are choosing it because it cannot be controlled by any government.

Regardless of people's individual reasons, this change is nevertheless happening — and it is happening now.

Will You Make The Change?

You can disregard the change happening to what we use as money. If you do, you risk being left behind — like those who held on to beads, salt or seashells.

Alternatively, you can learn about what is happening and then choose accordingly. If you do, you will be able to change along with our civilization and its money.

Changing Our Money Will Change the World

When our current form of money took over from gold, it changed the world — mostly, for the worse.

Bitcoin aims to remedy the problems that resulted from that change. It restores money's integrity. And, because money is so fundamental to a healthy, robust, and vibrant civilization, bitcoin can transform ours — to one that is sustainable, thriving, peaceful, honorable, productive, and rational.

Chapter 17

Why Bitcoin is the World's Most Inclusive Institution

Inclusivity is Good, But Hard

Eliminating unjust discrimination in institutions seems like an unwinnable war. We see case after case of powerful decisionmakers discriminating on the basis of factors like age, race, and gender. While we all know this is a problem, we do not know how to solve it.

We speak out against it, we protest, we pass laws, and we prosecute against it. However, in the end, the possibility of human irrationality means we can never entirely get rid of prejudice wherever people are in positions of power.

In Bitcoin Nobody is in Charge

Bitcoin offers a novel solution to the problem of unjust discrimination. Bitcoin's unique design means that nobody is in charge of any aspect of it – even deciding who can use it. By having no one in any role with the power to discriminate, bitcoin eliminates any and all possibility of such moral wickedness. Thus, it follows that everyone in the world can use bitcoin – regardless of anything at all, including their age, their race, and their gender.

No other institution in the world welcomes everybody to this degree. This makes bitcoin the world's most inclusive institution. You do not need an invitation. You do not need to live in any particular country.

You do not need a home address. You do not need photo identification.

You can use it without ever needing to tell bitcoin anything about yourself. In fact, you cannot even tell bitcoin anything about yourself!

Bitcoin Unites Us All

By making itself accessible to everyone in the world bitcoin becomes even more widely used every day. In the not-toodistant future, bitcoin may even become the most widely accepted money ever.

As there are no limits on who can use it, bitcoin can bring everyone in the world together. It connects those with nice homes to those with no shoes on their feet. It gathers together people of all races, all genders, all religions, all ideologies, all abilities — from all locations everywhere in the world.

Bitcoin unifies all mankind within one system — exhibiting incorruptible integrity, eliminating unjust discrimination, and guaranteeing equal treatment for all.

Chapter 18

Why Bitcoin Attracts Extraordinary Talent

Imagine If...

Imagine if a company existed which had great engineers and developers all volunteering to work for it out of their passion for its product. Imagine if they all also owned a part of it.

Suppose there were also philosophers, mathematicians, teachers, entrepreneurs, and risk-taking adventurers among all the volunteers. And, imagine if nobody took any salary.

No Bosses, Job Descriptions Or Discrimination

Why stop there? Imagine if this company had no structure – nobody hired or fired anybody, people would simply contribute what they could, whenever they could, full-time or part-time, permanently or temporarily. Literally anyone, anywhere in the world could join in, whenever they wanted – with no systemic discrimination of any kind.

There would also be no strategic plan, no job descriptions, no CEO – and no "Human Resources" department.

The Competition

Imagine if this company had competitors operating monopolies in every country on Earth. Each and every person was forced to use those competitors' products – which turn out to be nothing less than money itself!

But, their money is not good money. It is not money that holds its purchasing power. It is not money that resists confiscation. It is not money immune to being frozen. It is not money that takes any effort to create.

Yet, you must work hard for that money – while they do not. This is therefore a thoroughly unjust system of money. There is a great need for a just alternative. This is why so many people are volunteering to work for our imaginary company.

It is a company rooted in justice, because its product is actually sound money that holds its purchasing power, resists confiscation, is immune to being frozen – and does require effort to create.

Would You Join?

Ask yourself: Would you invest in this imaginary company? Would you participate in it? Would you use its product?

Multitudes of people would answer "Yes". Playing a role in creating desperately needed sound money would inspire, motivate and reward legions of diverse, smart and principled people.

You Can Join Us!

Now, of course there is no such company. Any company that tried to make sound money would get shut down in a heartbeat by governments, and its employees would be thrown in prison.

However, there is bitcoin. Bitcoin cannot be shut down. It is not a company. It has no CEO. It has no employees. It has no location. It has no "Compliance Department" to comply with any government's order to shut it down.

Bitcoin just runs on the efforts of volunteers – and on their computers.

However, bitcoin possesses all of the characteristics of our imaginary company that operates a just and desperately needed system of money.

Inspired by the incredible talent of its creator, Satoshi Nakamoto, and following in his footsteps, people from all walks of life and disciplines are drawn towards bitcoin's shining beacon of justice and freedom – eager to volunteer their unique and exceptional talents to its historic cause.

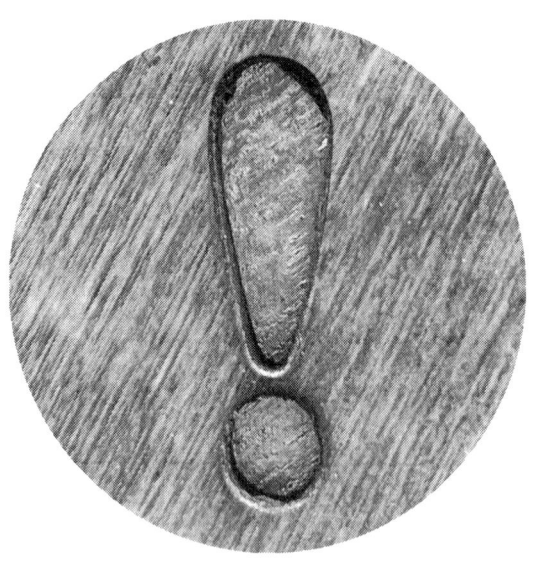

Chapter 19

Why You Shouldn't Fear Bitcoin

We Fear What May be Dangerous

The purpose of fear is to keep us away from what might harm us. However, we have no way of automatically knowing what will harm us. The unknown may be dangerous — or it may be beneficial. We need to discover which it is, and when.

A knife is a good example. It can be quite dangerous. When we learn to wield it properly, it becomes a tool we can use to prepare food, which is beneficial.

When we are young, we often fear knives, but with experience we come to view them as useful tools — and not as objects to fear.

Learning is a Gradual Process

The first time you tried to stand up, you fell down. With practice you got better. The same happened as you learned to walk and eventually to run. Walking was something you wanted to do. You could see other people doing it — and you could see the benefit of getting where you wanted.

When it came to learning even more skills, you may have wanted to learn some more than others — and that contributed to you becoming your unique self.

WHY BITCOIN?

People Say Frightening Things

Someone could have tried to scare you away from learning to run – maybe someone even did. "It's bad for your knees!" they might have warned. Some warnings are fair. But most are overblown. People can learn to run without damaging their knees.

Why Learn to Use Bitcoin

Bitcoin is a new form of something that just about every human being needs to use every day – money. Bitcoin is quickly becoming superior to all previous forms of money, including what we use now. It may already be the best way to save money for the future. And it is quickly becoming the most efficient and reliable way to send and receive money. Perhaps, most strikingly, it is the most secure form of money that has ever existed – in that it can never be confiscated or frozen.

You have nothing to fear from bitcoin. Do not let others scare you into believing that it is a "scheme" to take your money or that it is "dangerous to our environment". It is neither.

Like all new things, bitcoin takes time to understand. Fearing it before you understand it could lead you to mistakenly think it is dangerous – when it is actually beneficial.

Bitcoin is not an all-or-nothing bet. You can learn about it gradually. You can start with buying just a little. Then you can learn about it and experiment with it. If you mess up and lose this little bit, it could be like the first time you tried to stand up. Eventually, you will understand more and become more practiced. In time, you will become comfortable with it – just like you have with so many other things you learned.

Bitcoiners Will Guide You

You will find that the bitcoin community is incredibly eager to share what they have learned — and to help you on your journey. Bitcoiners are passionate about building a world with reliable, sound money.

They will explain, answer your questions, and try to protect you from hurting yourself.

In time, we hope you will benefit from the many advantages bitcoin offers. Perhaps you will become so inspired by these that you too will become one of bitcoin's many teachers — thereby helping other newcomers overcome their fears.

Chapter 20

Why Bitcoin is So Complicated

Do Not Blame bitcoin for Being Complicated

Bitcoin was born in 2009 into a very complicated world. It was a world of central banks – organizations that are not private, but also are not public. It was a world with over one quadrillion dollars of highly complicated financial "derivatives" – which exhibited extreme volatility causing multiple economic crises. It was a world where banks needed multiple "bailouts" – to save them from collapse.

Despite the many flaws of this system, those governments, politicians and bankers in charge are not about to let go of their control of money. And these people also control the police forces, laws, courts, tanks, drones, jet fighters and aircraft carriers.

For bitcoin to become the "good money" that Hayek talked about, it necessitated the use of "roundabout ways" which they could not stop.

Survival in a Complicated World

Bitcoin is the first and only system of money that cannot be stopped, taken over, confiscated, or broken by adversaries like governments, imitators, hackers, banks – or anything else.

In this undeniably complicated world, bitcoin needed to be a system that could survive those cruel, challenging, and adversarial conditons. It needed to be free from any leaders who could be threatened or bribed – so it opted to have no leaders. It needed to be free from any corruptible vulnerabilites — so it also left out anything that could possibly be compromised.

Bitcoin replaced all these exploitable vulnerabilites with rules based on incorruptible mathematics and inviolable laws of physics. Neither math nor physics can be stopped or overcome by man-made laws, by force, or by deception.

This is how bitcoin survives and defends itself from attacks by governments, hackers, and other opponents. It is the only way.

Everything Around Us is Complicated

Bitcoin is complicated because it needs to be. It relies only on proven principles of math and physics — and assembles them in an ingenious manner to fulfill all the requirements of "good money".

Bitcoin is not the only complicated thing we have to deal with. Computers are also very complicated — and few of us understand how they work. The same goes for automobiles, refrigerators, and the Internet.

Yet, those things work. The fact that they are complicated and complex does not stop us from using them.

Bitcoin's complexity is a necessity that should not stand in our way of using it. There is simply no other way to create the thing that Hayek "believed we might never have again" — good money.

Chapter 21

Why Bitcoin Can Handle All the Commerce in the World

Sending Money through Banks

Your bank holds your money. They also hold the money of many other people. When you send money to one of those people, the bank takes it out of your account and puts it in the other person's.

But your bank does not hold everyone's money. To send money to someone who banks elsewhere, your bank itself needs an account at that other person's bank. Then, your bank takes the money from you, and the other bank takes the same amount of money from them. Finally, their bank puts that money in the account of the person you are sending it to.

For this system to work, everyone needs to open accounts at banks. This business is very lucrative for banks – and makes them very powerful. This process can also be time-consuming, expensive – and often unreliable.

Bitcoin Frees Us from Banks

In bitcoin we eliminate the power that institutions have over us. We take back both the power and the money. Bitcoin's beauty is that it makes the previously impossible – possible.

We have already seen how it makes possible economic stability, increased purchasing power of savings, and the guaranteeing of equal treatment for everyone.

Lightning Bestows New Abilities on Bitcoin

The invention of bitcoin's "Lightning Network," first described in a whitepaper in 2016, introduces even more new possibilities – unlimited, instant, inexpensive transactions.

With Lightning, we do not need the banks anymore. We can send money to one another with each of us playing one of the roles the banks previously played.

If you and I are directly connected on bitcoin's Lightning Network, we can instantly send money back and forth to each other, at no cost, simply by updating our balances. And if you want to send money to someone only I am connected to, you can send it to me, and I will send it along to them – without anyone having to trust anyone. This only costs a tiny amount.

Lightning allows us to do all this instantly, securely, privately, cheaply – anytime, anywhere, with anyone.

Lightning Can Scale Infinitely

The more people who use Lightning, the more its capacity, speed, and reliability increases.

Just as the Internet scales infinitely when more routers, cables, switches, and servers are added, so too does the Lightning Network – except it scales through adding nodes, user connections, and bitcoins.

Even More Possibilities

Lightning goes even further. Since transactions are instant, cheap, and can be automated – and, since they can be tiny in value, the Lightning Network allows for previously unimaginable applications.

Uses like streaming money by the second to avoid pre-authorizations, and pay-as-you-go for anything — or instant international remittances for purchases ranging in size from a cup of coffee, to a basket of groceries — to a mortgage payment.

Lightning's potential is limited only by the imaginations of bitcoin's brilliant, creative and growing community. As their innovations roll out, bitcoin's Lightning Network can scale to meet all the demands of a thriving and growing global civilization.

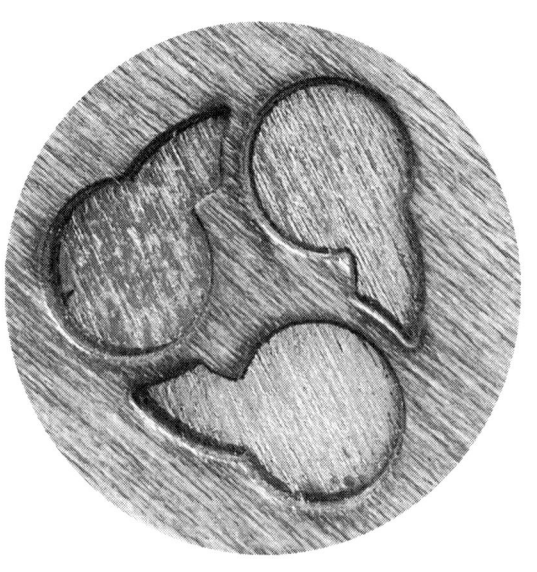

Chapter 22

Why Bitcoin's Imitators Are Scams

The Sincerest Form of Flattery

Bitcoin has many imitators — none as good. The most common mistake newcomers make is falling for the false claim that any of these imitators represent an improvement on bitcoin. These scams go by the name of "Crypto".

Bitcoin is an invention of profound ingenuity — providing sound, incorruptible money to everyone in the world.

However, as we have seen, bitcoin is complicated. It is also new. And there is much money at stake. These facts attract predators seeking to separate newcomers from their money.

Since bitcoin itself is incorruptible, these scammers must trick their victims into handing over money for something other than bitcoin. These frauds do so by creating imitations of bitcoin. Sadly, they have gotten away with tricking many would-be bitcoiners into buying these fundamentally worthless "alternatives".

Don't Trust, Verify!

How are you to know if these imitators' claims of being better are valid? Granted, this is not easy, but there is a credo bitcoiners use that gets to the very core:

"Don't trust. Verify."

WHY BITCOIN?

Every single aspect of bitcoin is independently verifiable. You can validate every transaction, every block – even every line of programming. This makes bitcoin incorruptible – and "trustless".

"You Can Trust Me"

The strategy of "crypto" con-artists is to obtain your confidence with bogus or irrelevant claims. They then betray that trust by giving you bogus or irrelevant digital tokens in exchange for your hard-earned money. Curiously enough, these scammers will themselves often want bitcoin for their tokens – which, right there, should tell you everything you need to know.

The typical "crypto" scam thus almost always has a smooth-talking, charismatic character at its helm. Whether it is a boy genius who speaks in incomprehensible techno-jargon, a libertarian rebel, a guy in a business suit with a nice accent, or someone dressed up like a magician – if there is someone in charge who you have to trust, that is who is going to take your money. The tokens that they are selling you cost them nothing to create.

Trust No One

Any "crypto" which has spokespeople, leaders, or institutes must put its trust in these people – and therefore, so also must you. As a result, that "crypto" lacks the singlemost important feature at the heart of bitcoin – incorruptibily.

Bitcoin Puts no Trust in any Human Beings – "Cryptos" Do.

Anything claiming to be "better" than bitcoin because it is newer, or has allegedly improved on some feature of it, seeks to lure you away from what truly matters most.

Why Bitcoin's Imitators Are Scams

Bells and whistles are irrelevant — trustlessness is the only important and necessary test.

Anything that relies on trust in some group of human beings is therefore not a step forward from bitcoin, but rather a step backwards that reintroduces the old problems bitcoin solved.

Bitcoin puts trust in nobody. That is the genius of its invention. It is a system free from trust in mere human beings. You yourself can read bitcoin's whitepaper and with a bit of effort understand how bitcoin works to achieve trustlessness. Bitcoin is the only trustless-money technology.

But don't take my word for it.

Verify!

Chapter 23

Why Bitcoin is So Much More Than Money

Cars Changed the World

Cars turned out to be so much more than just another way to get around. Automobiles didn't simply replace the horse and buggy. Rather, they ushered in a new age – one of massive mobility. Billions of people could now safely move about at high speeds – and at any time. This led to an explosion in the number of places that people could go.

Cars made it possible for many new things to exist and thrive: shopping malls, movie theaters, theme parks, vacation homes, suburbs, and so much more. Cars liberated people and the result was profoundly transformational on the lives of everyone. Cars changed the world.

However, in the early days of the automobile it was not obvious that any of this would happen. Back then, cars were not faster than horses. They were vastly outnumbered by horses. Roads were not designed for them. No highways existed. In time, all that changed.

Now It is Bitcoin's Turn

This same phenomenon is happening again – this time with money. Bitcoin is a massive improvement over all previous forms of money in every respect. It is secure, scarce and accessible to everyone in the world. It can be sent anywhere. It lasts forever. It is predictable, auditable, verifiable, and divisible. It is, to put it simply, profoundly superior.

WHY BITCOIN?

Bitcoin's buildout will be as profound as was the buildout for cars. Cars led to an abundance of paved roads, highways, gas stations, car makers, the assembly line, and more. Bitcoin will also lead to a transformation of our society. Just as cars are everywhere now, bitcoin will be everywhere soon. It will be sent instantly and cheaply to anyone, anywhere. It will enable previously impossible trade relationships. It will replace today's primitive financial institutions.

As this transformation happens, bitcoin will liberate people. It will free us to store and transfer money without banks. It will free us from inflation that destroys our savings – and which forces unhealthy over-consumption. It will free us from the costs of converting money across international borders. It will free us from tremendous debts. It will free us from the countless constraints of today's financial system.

When bitcoin achieves mass adoption, our civilization will advance as dramatically as it did when automobiles ended the horse and buggy era.

Bitcoin will make possible countless new ideas which were previously unimaginable. Please – do not limit your thinking of bitcoin merely to it being a new type of money. Instead, recognize and appreciate that it is so much more – an invention that will change the world.

Chapter 24

Why You Need Bitcoin

You are Truly Magnificent!

You are a once in the history of the Universe event. Nothing quite like you ever existed before. And, when you are gone, nothing exactly like you will ever again exist.

When you are truly being yourself, nobody else can do what you do in the unique way which only you can. Nobody can appreciate the joy of being you as much as you can. You are special, wonderful, and extraordinary.

You have a purpose. Discovering and fulfilling this purpose will give you great joy. There is no other feeling like it. Please – take ten seconds now to reflect on how much, deep down within, you truly do love yourself. Next, please take ten seconds more to consider just how profoundly you desire to fully express yourself.

The Secret to True Wealth

We now have the resources to build a world in which you can live long enough and with enough wealth to fulfill that desire. This is not the kind of wealth that exists for showing off how much money you have. Such displays are mere pretenses at wealth – they contribute nothing to you being yourself. Our civilization can produce so much wealth that each of us can pursue our true purpose.

This is the real feeling of being wealthy – it is the feeling of freedom.

Claim Your Freedom!

However, there is a problem. Your freedom is restricted by powers that control money and who, through that control, are your masters – and you their slave.

If masters and rulers preside over you – and if they can seize or negate the results of your efforts – you can not exercise your necessary freedoms.

Instead, you are forced into anticipating their whims or obeying their orders – making you their puppet. Or, you must plead with them to bestow their favors upon you – making you a beggar. But you are neither a puppet nor a beggar. You are a magnificent, heroic human being – and bitcoin frees you from these tormentors' chains!

Bitcoin is the key to you taking back control of your life. It gives you the power to ensure the choices you make about what do with your time and energy – will be choices you can count on. Your bitcoin can not be controlled by anybody else – no matter how rich or how powerful. It is yours to do with as you freely choose.

To become your truly magnificent self – and to remain so – you need bitcoin!

Chapter 25

Why Bitcoin is the New Frontier

Once, it was the "new world" that represented the new frontier. Then, after the Americas were settled, we believed space was the next and final frontier.

Now, we have a radically new frontier which beckons our attention — bitcoin.

For those with the curiosity to heed its call, bitcoin has emerged as a vast and mysterious space to explore — offering us legendary treasures, thrilling adventures, and unlimited potential.

As promised in the Statue of Liberty's beautiful — but sadly no longer true invitation — bitcoin invites those who are tired, poor and yearning to breathe free to enter its realm and bask in the light of its gifts.

The bitcoin frontier exists throughout the entire Earth. It allows human civilization to surge forward into undeveloped territory.

This new frontier is accessible to anyone, anywhere, anytime. It rewards its explorers for discovering new sources of energy. It encourages them to focus on long time horizons. It liberates them from the arbitrary decrees of soul-sucking institutions.

As with any new frontier, though, the going is not always easy. The exploration and development involve hard work, difficult challenges, extreme patience, and even danger to life and limb. However, its rewards offer a reclamation of lost liberties, and even a discovery of new freedoms essential for human thriving. These values have long been disappearing from our world.

Yet, to those who choose bitcoin, these freedoms are well worth the efforts and the risks required to reclaim and reconstruct them – this time in an indestructible manner.

Bitcoin gets better with time through effort, and it is open to everyone – whenever they choose.

So, we sojourn forth into this new frontier – bravely, curiously, openly, and transparently – and we invite the world to watch us, and to join us.

Chapter 26

Why Bitcoin is Worthy of Your Love

There is a saying that "the love of money is the root of all evil". And bitcoin is money. However, bitcoin is reliable, sound, honest money — and, as such, it is good for you, for humanity, and for the planet.

What is Love?

How is love earned and sustained?

To be loved, one must offer something of uniqely irreplaceable value.

One must also never taint the love through betraying that value.

One must be honest — allowing oneself to be evaluated without concealment. Anything less than complete transparency might be hiding something which undermines that love.

Bitcoin is Worthy

Bitcoin says to every individual on Earth:

"I offer you the greatest instrument for money that has ever existed — bitcoin.

"My nature ensures this money's supply is limited and always verifiable to you. This money cannot be taken from you by force. You can send any of yours to whomever you want — for any reason. This money can store the efforts of your work for any length of time — including a time beyond your own life or the existence of your country.

WHY BITCOIN?

"I am bound to keep these assurances by the inviolable laws of math and physics.

"Look upon me and you can verify all my claims. I do not ask for your trust. I hide nothing. I stand before you naked, open, and transparent. My programming is open and public. My history is public. You are welcome to keep copies of these and always verify their accuracy.

"If you find any flaw in my claims, you may change me. But the change must truly correct me, for I am watched over by millions of others — and they will prevent any change to me that will betray my promises.

"I will never reject you, under any circumstances, no matter what actions you have taken before. I am here to be judged, but I do not judge you.

"I will never force you to accept me, let alone to love me. I will always remain here with my offer to you of all this. And, I await, patiently — until you are ready."

Chapter 27

Why Bitcoin is a Movement of Peace

THIS IS A DECLARATION OF PEACE!

I will not fight you.
Because *I* do not need to.
I do not *want* to fight you.
One of us might get hurt, or even *killed*, – and it might be *me*.
But, if I needed to, I *would*.
Thankfully, for *both* our sakes, I do not.

There is yet a *nobler* reason behind my *not* wanting to fight you.
I want to work *with* you.
So that I can show you the best of *me*, and you can show me the best of *you*.
I want to co-exist in *peace* with you.
Thanks to bitcoin, I can.

Those who do not know bitcoin, may wonder why solely *my* knowledge of bitcoin suffices for *me* to declare peace unto *them*.
Shalom. Salaam.
The reason is that I have a *shield*.
My wealth can *not* be stolen.
So I do not view *others* as a threat.
If they assert themselves as my enemy, I simply laugh them off.
What *can* they do to me?
They gain *nothing* by hurting me.
If they kill me – they do *not* get my bitcoin.

WHY BITCOIN?

And I want *nothing* from anyone that they do not freely want to exchange with me.
That is because I am a bitcoiner – I *embrace* bitcoin, the inviolable system which *only* permits consensual exchange.

Bitcoin is money that can *never* be stolen from one who wields it responsibly.
And *I* have learned to wield it responsibly.
It is *not* a weapon, but a *shield*.
I can not use it to *hurt* you.
And you can not use it to *hurt* me.

So I declare peace unto you!
Whether or not you are ready for peace with me.
Mine is a unilateral declaration.
I yearn for the day when you declare the same.

Will you take my hand and embrace me in peace?
I would *rejoice* in it!
But I can wait – if you are not yet ready.
I have all the time in the world.
I have bitcoin.

Who *else* am I declaring peace upon?
Every single person and nation in the whole wide world.
And also every government and every company.

What are my terms?
I have *none*.
Anyone may turn their back to me.
I will initiate *no* violence upon them.

So what then?" you may object, "there is *nothing* in your offer of peace."

Quite the *opposite* is true.
Let me tell you what is in my offer.
First, I offer the Shield to *everyone*.
I need *not* surrender it.
I will *forever* have it with me.
But, it is *expansive* and can protect countless human lives.
So I give it *willingly* to you all, which costs me *nothing* — but bestows upon us all a *tremendous* value.

So take it.
It is also *yours*.
It awaits for whenever *you* are ready.
I will *not* force this Shield upon you, for I come in peace.
No man who attempts to *force* you is with me.
It must be *your* choice.
You *raise* the Shield in an act of self-respect and self-assertion — to say:
"What is mine is mine and no man may take it from me!"

I offer to *guide* you on how to wield it so that it *truly* works as I have promised.
I will show you how to *know* this for yourself — without you needing to *trust* me.
I also offer you the very best I have to give.
That, however, I do not offer for free.
I offer it in *trade*.
So let us trade.
Let us do so *honestly* and *rationally*.
Let us treat each other with *respect* and *decency*.
Let us form a *lifelong* relationship for our *mutual* benefit.
If we can not, that, too, is fine.
We can leave each other in peace, and find *many* others with whom to trade.

I do not come *alone*.

WHY BITCOIN?

With me are *all* the others who have taken up the Shield.
We are not perfect.
But we are good.
And we each wish to *work* to make this world *better* through *peaceful* trade of the best we each have to offer.
Haven't you been *searching* for us all along?
We are here.
We are ready.
We are ready to think.
We are ready to work.
We are ready to trade.
Honestly and rationally, together – with *you*.
We are a multitude, but *not* an army.
For we come in peace.
Will you join us?

We are the *free* and *peaceful* people of Earth and, if you will have us, we welcome you!
We will *respect* your decision, whatever it is, and be at peace with you – whatever your choice.
What *greater* cause can you think of than freedom and peace?
And honesty, and respect?
And – perhaps even *love*?

Ours is not some fanciful, naive, and feeble-minded movement of *weaknesses* and *wishes*!
We *know* we have to work.
We know we have to *grasp* reality and work in harmony with it.
We do not expect something for nothing.
But we also do not expect *nothing* in exchange for something.
Those who offer us nothing in exchange for our effort – we simply leave in peace.
And we welcome them at *any* time if they wish to offer *us* something instead of nothing.

Our pursuits are happiness, longevity and love. Do *not* laugh at this. Should that not be *each* person's pursuit? Look *deep* within yourself. Is that not what *you* desire too? We *can* find it, *together* — in peace.

— Tomer Strolight

Bitcoin: A Peer-to-Peer Electronic Cash System

Satoshi Nakamoto
satoshin@gmx.com
www.bitcoin.org

Abstract. A purely peer-to-peer version of electronic cash would allow online payments to be sent directly from one party to another without going through a financial institution. Digital signatures provide part of the solution, but the main benefits are lost if a trusted third party is still required to prevent double-spending. We propose a solution to the double-spending problem using a peer-to-peer network. The network timestamps transactions by hashing them into an ongoing chain of hash-based proof-of-work, forming a record that cannot be changed without redoing the proof-of-work. The longest chain not only serves as proof of the sequence of events witnessed, but proof that it came from the largest pool of CPU power. As long as a majority of CPU power is controlled by nodes that are not cooperating to attack the network, they'll generate the longest chain and outpace attackers. The network itself requires minimal structure. Messages are broadcast on a best effort basis, and nodes can leave and rejoin the network at will, accepting the longest proof-of-work chain as proof of what happened while they were gone.

1. Introduction

Commerce on the Internet has come to rely almost exclusively on financial institutions serving as trusted third parties to process electronic payments. While the system works well enough for most transactions, it still suffers from the inherent weaknesses of the trust based model. Completely non-reversible transactions are not really possible, since financial institutions cannot avoid mediating disputes. The cost of mediation increases transaction costs, limiting the minimum practical transaction size and cutting off the possibility for small casual transactions, and there is a broader cost in the loss of ability to make non-reversible payments for non-reversible services. With the possibility of reversal, the need for trust spreads. Merchants must be wary of their customers, hassling them for more information than they would otherwise need. A certain percentage of fraud is accepted as unavoidable. These costs and payment uncertainties can be avoided in person by using physical currency, but no mechanism exists to make payments over a communications channel without a trusted party.

What is needed is an electronic payment system based on cryptographic proof instead of trust, allowing any two willing parties to transact directly with each other without the need for a trusted third party. Transactions that are computationally impractical to reverse would protect sellers from fraud, and routine escrow mechanisms could easily be implemented to protect buyers. In this paper, we propose a solution to the double-spending problem using a peer-to-peer distributed timestamp server to generate computational proof of the chronological order of transactions. The system is secure as long as honest nodes collectively control more CPU power than any cooperating group of attacker nodes.

2. Transactions

We define an electronic coin as a chain of digital signatures. Each owner transfers the coin to the next by digitally signing a hash of the previous transaction and the public key of the next owner and adding these to the end of the coin. A payee can verify the signatures to verify the chain of ownership.

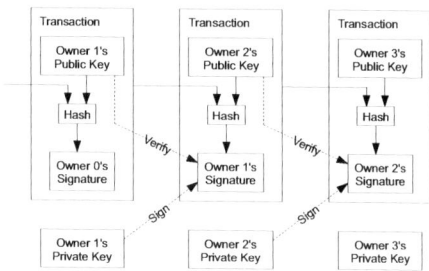

The problem of course is the payee can't verify that one of the owners did not double-spend the coin. A common solution is to introduce a trusted central authority, or mint, that checks every transaction for double spending. After each transaction, the coin must be returned to the mint to issue a new coin, and only coins issued directly from the mint are trusted not to be double-spent. The problem with this solution is that the fate of the entire money system depends on the company running the mint, with every transaction having to go through them, just like a bank.

We need a way for the payee to know that the previous owners did not sign any earlier transactions. For our purposes, the earliest transaction is the one that counts, so we don't care about later attempts to double-spend. The only way to confirm the absence of a transaction is to be aware of all transactions. In the mint based model, the mint was aware of all transactions and decided which arrived first. To accomplish this without a trusted party, transactions must be publicly announced [1], and we need a system for participants to agree on a single history of the order in which they were received. The payee needs proof that at the time of each transaction, the majority of nodes agreed it was the first received.

3. Timestamp Server

The solution we propose begins with a timestamp server. A timestamp server works by taking a hash of a block of items to be timestamped and widely publishing the hash, such as in a newspaper or Usenet post [2-5]. The timestamp proves that the data must have existed at the time, obviously, in order to get into the hash. Each timestamp includes the previous timestamp in its hash, forming a chain, with each additional timestamp reinforcing the ones before it.

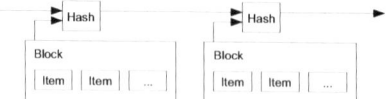

4. Proof-of-Work

To implement a distributed timestamp server on a peer-to-peer basis, we will need to use a proof-of-work system similar to Adam Back's Hashcash [6], rather than newspaper or Usenet posts. The proof-of-work involves scanning for a value that when hashed, such as with SHA-256, the hash begins with a number of zero bits. The average work required is exponential in the number of zero bits required and can be verified by executing a single hash.

For our timestamp network, we implement the proof-of-work by incrementing a nonce in the block until a value is found that gives the block's hash the required zero bits. Once the CPU effort has been expended to make it satisfy the proof-of-work, the block cannot be changed without redoing the work. As later blocks are chained after it, the work to change the block would include redoing all the blocks after it.

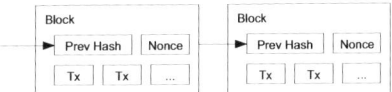

The proof-of-work also solves the problem of determining representation in majority decision making. If the majority were based on one-IP-address-one-vote, it could be subverted by anyone able to allocate many IPs. Proof-of-work is essentially one-CPU-one-vote. The majority decision is represented by the longest chain, which has the greatest proof-of-work effort invested in it. If a majority of CPU power is controlled by honest nodes, the honest chain will grow the fastest and outpace any competing chains. To modify a past block, an attacker would have to redo the proof-of-work of the block and all blocks after it and then catch up with and surpass the work of the honest nodes. We will show later that the probability of a slower attacker catching up diminishes exponentially as subsequent blocks are added.

To compensate for increasing hardware speed and varying interest in running nodes over time, the proof-of-work difficulty is determined by a moving average targeting an average number of blocks per hour. If they're generated too fast, the difficulty increases.

5. Network

The steps to run the network are as follows:

1) New transactions are broadcast to all nodes.
2) Each node collects new transactions into a block.
3) Each node works on finding a difficult proof-of-work for its block.
4) When a node finds a proof-of-work, it broadcasts the block to all nodes.
5) Nodes accept the block only if all transactions in it are valid and not already spent.
6) Nodes express their acceptance of the block by working on creating the next block in the chain, using the hash of the accepted block as the previous hash.

Nodes always consider the longest chain to be the correct one and will keep working on extending it. If two nodes broadcast different versions of the next block simultaneously, some nodes may receive one or the other first. In that case, they work on the first one they received, but save the other branch in case it becomes longer. The tie will be broken when the next proof-of-work is found and one branch becomes longer; the nodes that were working on the other branch will then switch to the longer one.

New transaction broadcasts do not necessarily need to reach all nodes. As long as they reach many nodes, they will get into a block before long. Block broadcasts are also tolerant of dropped messages. If a node does not receive a block, it will request it when it receives the next block and realizes it missed one.

6. Incentive

By convention, the first transaction in a block is a special transaction that starts a new coin owned by the creator of the block. This adds an incentive for nodes to support the network, and provides a way to initially distribute coins into circulation, since there is no central authority to issue them. The steady addition of a constant of amount of new coins is analogous to gold miners expending resources to add gold to circulation. In our case, it is CPU time and electricity that is expended.

The incentive can also be funded with transaction fees. If the output value of a transaction is less than its input value, the difference is a transaction fee that is added to the incentive value of the block containing the transaction. Once a predetermined number of coins have entered circulation, the incentive can transition entirely to transaction fees and be completely inflation free.

The incentive may help encourage nodes to stay honest. If a greedy attacker is able to assemble more CPU power than all the honest nodes, he would have to choose between using it to defraud people by stealing back his payments, or using it to generate new coins. He ought to find it more profitable to play by the rules, such rules that favour him with more new coins than everyone else combined, than to undermine the system and the validity of his own wealth.

7. Reclaiming Disk Space

Once the latest transaction in a coin is buried under enough blocks, the spent transactions before it can be discarded to save disk space. To facilitate this without breaking the block's hash, transactions are hashed in a Merkle Tree [7][2][5], with only the root included in the block's hash. Old blocks can then be compacted by stubbing off branches of the tree. The interior hashes do not need to be stored.

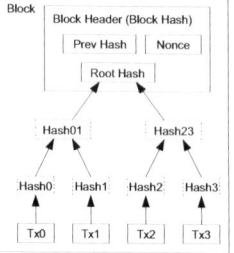
Transactions Hashed in a Merkle Tree

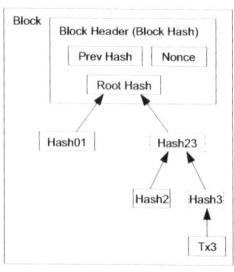
After Pruning Tx0-2 from the Block

A block header with no transactions would be about 80 bytes. If we suppose blocks are generated every 10 minutes, 80 bytes * 6 * 24 * 365 = 4.2MB per year. With computer systems typically selling with 2GB of RAM as of 2008, and Moore's Law predicting current growth of 1.2GB per year, storage should not be a problem even if the block headers must be kept in memory.

8. Simplified Payment Verification

It is possible to verify payments without running a full network node. A user only needs to keep a copy of the block headers of the longest proof-of-work chain, which he can get by querying network nodes until he's convinced he has the longest chain, and obtain the Merkle branch linking the transaction to the block it's timestamped in. He can't check the transaction for himself, but by linking it to a place in the chain, he can see that a network node has accepted it, and blocks added after it further confirm the network has accepted it.

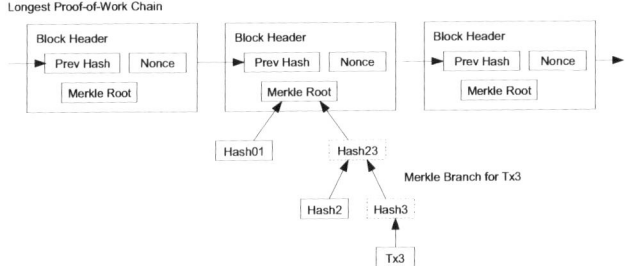

As such, the verification is reliable as long as honest nodes control the network, but is more vulnerable if the network is overpowered by an attacker. While network nodes can verify transactions for themselves, the simplified method can be fooled by an attacker's fabricated transactions for as long as the attacker can continue to overpower the network. One strategy to protect against this would be to accept alerts from network nodes when they detect an invalid block, prompting the user's software to download the full block and alerted transactions to confirm the inconsistency. Businesses that receive frequent payments will probably still want to run their own nodes for more independent security and quicker verification.

9. Combining and Splitting Value

Although it would be possible to handle coins individually, it would be unwieldy to make a separate transaction for every cent in a transfer. To allow value to be split and combined, transactions contain multiple inputs and outputs. Normally there will be either a single input from a larger previous transaction or multiple inputs combining smaller amounts, and at most two outputs: one for the payment, and one returning the change, if any, back to the sender.

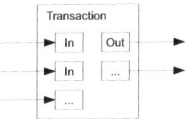

It should be noted that fan-out, where a transaction depends on several transactions, and those transactions depend on many more, is not a problem here. There is never the need to extract a complete standalone copy of a transaction's history.

10. Privacy

The traditional banking model achieves a level of privacy by limiting access to information to the parties involved and the trusted third party. The necessity to announce all transactions publicly precludes this method, but privacy can still be maintained by breaking the flow of information in another place: by keeping public keys anonymous. The public can see that someone is sending an amount to someone else, but without information linking the transaction to anyone. This is similar to the level of information released by stock exchanges, where the time and size of individual trades, the "tape", is made public, but without telling who the parties were.

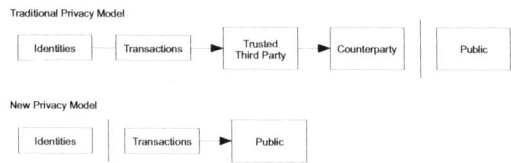

As an additional firewall, a new key pair should be used for each transaction to keep them from being linked to a common owner. Some linking is still unavoidable with multi-input transactions, which necessarily reveal that their inputs were owned by the same owner. The risk is that if the owner of a key is revealed, linking could reveal other transactions that belonged to the same owner.

11. Calculations

We consider the scenario of an attacker trying to generate an alternate chain faster than the honest chain. Even if this is accomplished, it does not throw the system open to arbitrary changes, such as creating value out of thin air or taking money that never belonged to the attacker. Nodes are not going to accept an invalid transaction as payment, and honest nodes will never accept a block containing them. An attacker can only try to change one of his own transactions to take back money he recently spent.

The race between the honest chain and an attacker chain can be characterized as a Binomial Random Walk. The success event is the honest chain being extended by one block, increasing its lead by +1, and the failure event is the attacker's chain being extended by one block, reducing the gap by -1.

The probability of an attacker catching up from a given deficit is analogous to a Gambler's Ruin problem. Suppose a gambler with unlimited credit starts at a deficit and plays potentially an infinite number of trials to try to reach breakeven. We can calculate the probability he ever reaches breakeven, or that an attacker ever catches up with the honest chain, as follows [8]:

p = probability an honest node finds the next block
q = probability the attacker finds the next block
q_z = probability the attacker will ever catch up from z blocks behind

$$q_z = \begin{cases} 1 & if\ p \leq q \\ (q/p)^z & if\ p > q \end{cases}$$

Given our assumption that $p > q$, the probability drops exponentially as the number of blocks the attacker has to catch up with increases. With the odds against him, if he doesn't make a lucky lunge forward early on, his chances become vanishingly small as he falls further behind.

We now consider how long the recipient of a new transaction needs to wait before being sufficiently certain the sender can't change the transaction. We assume the sender is an attacker who wants to make the recipient believe he paid him for a while, then switch it to pay back to himself after some time has passed. The receiver will be alerted when that happens, but the sender hopes it will be too late.

The receiver generates a new key pair and gives the public key to the sender shortly before signing. This prevents the sender from preparing a chain of blocks ahead of time by working on it continuously until he is lucky enough to get far enough ahead, then executing the transaction at that moment. Once the transaction is sent, the dishonest sender starts working in secret on a parallel chain containing an alternate version of his transaction.

The recipient waits until the transaction has been added to a block and z blocks have been linked after it. He doesn't know the exact amount of progress the attacker has made, but assuming the honest blocks took the average expected time per block, the attacker's potential progress will be a Poisson distribution with expected value:

$$\lambda = z \frac{q}{p}$$

To get the probability the attacker could still catch up now, we multiply the Poisson density for each amount of progress he could have made by the probability he could catch up from that point:

$$\sum_{k=0}^{\infty} \frac{\lambda^k e^{-\lambda}}{k!} \cdot \begin{cases} (q/p)^{(z-k)} & \text{if } k \leq z \\ 1 & \text{if } k > z \end{cases}$$

Rearranging to avoid summing the infinite tail of the distribution...

$$1 - \sum_{k=0}^{z} \frac{\lambda^k e^{-\lambda}}{k!} \left(1 - (q/p)^{(z-k)}\right)$$

Converting to C code...

```c
#include <math.h>
double AttackerSuccessProbability(double q, int z)
{
    double p = 1.0 - q;
    double lambda = z * (q / p);
    double sum = 1.0;
    int i, k;
    for (k = 0; k <= z; k++)
    {
        double poisson = exp(-lambda);
        for (i = 1; i <= k; i++)
            poisson *= lambda / i;
        sum -= poisson * (1 - pow(q / p, z - k));
    }
    return sum;
}
```

Running some results, we can see the probability drop off exponentially with z.

```
q=0.1
  z=0      P=1.0000000
  z=1      P=0.2045873
  z=2      P=0.0509779
  z=3      P=0.0131722
  z=4      P=0.0034552
  z=5      P=0.0009137
  z=6      P=0.0002428
  z=7      P=0.0000647
  z=8      P=0.0000173
  z=9      P=0.0000046
  z=10     P=0.0000012

q=0.3
  z=0      P=1.0000000
  z=5      P=0.1773523
  z=10     P=0.0416605
  z=15     P=0.0101008
  z=20     P=0.0024804
  z=25     P=0.0006132
  z=30     P=0.0001522
  z=35     P=0.0000379
  z=40     P=0.0000095
  z=45     P=0.0000024
  z=50     P=0.0000006
```

Solving for P less than 0.1%...

```
P < 0.001
  q=0.10    z=5
  q=0.15    z=8
  q=0.20    z=11
  q=0.25    z=15
  q=0.30    z=24
  q=0.35    z=41
  q=0.40    z=89
  q=0.45    z=340
```

12. Conclusion

We have proposed a system for electronic transactions without relying on trust. We started with the usual framework of coins made from digital signatures, which provides strong control of ownership, but is incomplete without a way to prevent double-spending. To solve this, we proposed a peer-to-peer network using proof-of-work to record a public history of transactions that quickly becomes computationally impractical for an attacker to change if honest nodes control a majority of CPU power. The network is robust in its unstructured simplicity. Nodes work all at once with little coordination. They do not need to be identified, since messages are not routed to any particular place and only need to be delivered on a best effort basis. Nodes can leave and rejoin the network at will, accepting the proof-of-work chain as proof of what happened while they were gone. They vote with their CPU power, expressing their acceptance of valid blocks by working on extending them and rejecting invalid blocks by refusing to work on them. Any needed rules and incentives can be enforced with this consensus mechanism.

References

[1] W. Dai, "b-money," http://www.weidai.com/bmoney.txt, 1998.

[2] H. Massias, X.S. Avila, and J.-J. Quisquater, "Design of a secure timestamping service with minimal trust requirements," In *20th Symposium on Information Theory in the Benelux*, May 1999.

[3] S. Haber, W.S. Stornetta, "How to time-stamp a digital document," In *Journal of Cryptology*, vol 3, no 2, pages 99-111, 1991.

[4] D. Bayer, S. Haber, W.S. Stornetta, "Improving the efficiency and reliability of digital time-stamping," In *Sequences II: Methods in Communication, Security and Computer Science*, pages 329-334, 1993.

[5] S. Haber, W.S. Stornetta, "Secure names for bit-strings," In *Proceedings of the 4th ACM Conference on Computer and Communications Security*, pages 28-35, April 1997.

[6] A. Back, "Hashcash - a denial of service counter-measure," http://www.hashcash.org/papers/hashcash.pdf, 2002.

[7] R.C. Merkle, "Protocols for public key cryptosystems," In *Proc. 1980 Symposium on Security and Privacy*, IEEE Computer Society, pages 122-133, April 1980.

[8] W. Feller, "An introduction to probability theory and its applications," 1957.

More from the Author

Essays on Bitcoin

www.medium.com/@TomerStrolight

www.Swan.com/signal

www.bitcoinmagazine.com/authors/tomer-strolight

Bitcoin Fiction

"Satoshi and Me" at www.Citadel21.com/satoshi-and-me

"The Being That Changed Everything" on The Bitcoin Times at

www.medium.com/the-bitcoin-times

"Moving Heaven and Earth" at www.medium.com/@TomerStrolight

Video

"Bitcoin Is Generational Wealth" on Swan Signal channel on YouTube: https://youtu.be/3Rnqst5qCgA

Printed in Poland
by Amazon Fulfillment
Poland Sp. z o.o., Wrocław
04 June 2024

f8bc5751-2130-47da-8758-1940e97cae09R01